To Mike
Ponder every
chance you get!

A Time to... Ponder

Reflections on Ecclesiastics 3:1-8

Sylvia Casberg

Sunny Fields Publishing
2162 Creekside Drive, Solvang, CA 93463-2239

Book design by Sylvia Casberg

First edition

ISBN   978-0-9827781-3-5

~

Dedication

To my teachers
from pre-school through graduate school,
from the school of hard knocks
through continuing education,
thank you so much.

Other books by Sylvia Casberg

A Christmas Passing

Praying the Seasons

Shadows from the Cross

Table of Contents

Thoughts from the Author

This passage of scripture from The Hebrew Bible has been the most requested spiritual reading in my thirty-five years of ministry.

It makes no difference whether people attend worship or walk by on the street, they know this scripture. It makes no difference whether they are Christian, Jew, Muslim or Buddhist, they know this scripture, and its wisdom speaks to them.

Ecclesiastics 3:1-8 is requested for weddings, baptisms, graduations, retirements, and funerals, any occasion marking a passage.

It is for this audience I have written an earthy, authentic, poetic meditation. It speaks to anyone pondering the ambiguities of life.

Sylvia Casberg

8

Ecclesiastes 3:1-8

For everything there is a season,
and a time for every matter under heaven:

a time to be born,
and a time to die;

a time to plant,
and a time to pluck up what is planted;

a time to kill,
and a time to heal;

a time to break down,
and a time to build up;

a time to weep,
and a time to laugh;

a time to mourn,
and a time to dance;

a time to throw away stones,
and a time to gather stones together;

a time to embrace,
and a time to refrain from embracing;

a time to seek,
and a time to lose;

a time to keep,
and a time to throw away;

a time to tear,
and a time to sew;

a time to keep silence,
and a time to speak;

a time to love,
and a time to hate;

a time for war,
and a time for peace.

A TIME TO BE BORN

I choose life. This is my time to be born, to live, laugh, move and have my being. This is life after birth, a time unmeasured, a span of days for me to live as I will, no matter how many or how few. A time to feel cold winds and warm fires, to smell supper cooking and summer's lawn in the mowing. A time to touch babies' cheeks and lovers' bellies, to hear the climax of a great symphony and morning's bell to prayer. A time to taste chocolate and cream, and burn my tongue on afternoon tea. A time to see my beloved's face across the breakfast table, and wrap our day in dreams.

Each morning is a birth. From the labor of night comes the delivery of each new day, fresh-faced and curious, waiting for lines of character to be drawn across the hours until sunset. From the gift of spirit, energy bubbles up in my soul like the fermenting of a fine wine. It pours into each day, and all these days are gathered up into a lifetime of sacramental living.

It is time to live every moment, humble or grand. Time to relish the rhythm of breath, the company of good friends, the luxury of Sunday afternoon naps. It is time to savor the quiet glory of morning and the grace of evening, the noise of children and the quiet of old folks reliving favorite memories.

The rhythm of birth beats through the seasons of my life, slowing down here and there so I may delight in moments of re-birth. It speeds up to meet the demands of adrenaline days, always reminding me of my mortality and that fragile thread by which life hangs. The rhythm of birth beats a story of beginnings, learning to sleep in strange beds, attend new schools, begin new jobs, meet new people. I begin to trust this pattern. I know I can fail and try again, make a fool of myself and forgive myself.

I can trust some people, and others not; make terrible mistakes and survive; confront tragedy and death and eventually come back into rebirth. My rhythm beats...begin and begin and begin. Be not afraid. Be not afraid. Be not afraid.

Birth isn't pleasant at first, but to live, really live, I need to keep being born. I need to keep learning new things. I want to gorge my senses, stuff my mind, and fill my soul's cup until it runs over and over and over. To keep my eyes open until they water, because if I blink I might miss something. To taste everything, especially peaches picked on warm afternoons, juice rolling down my cheeks and neck and arms. To feel skin against mine on cold nights when we can't hold each other tightly enough. To hear music and thrill to each crescendo. To smell gardenias from a moonlit garden, their scent drifting through my bedroom window and into my dreams.

I want to be a glutton at life's banquet table.

14

~

God of celebration, come dance with me.

Sing of life and challenge and fine wine

lifted

in

Eucharistic living!

16

A TIME TO DIE

Some day I'm going to die. I will actually be gone, my life finished and forgotten. A date will mark my passing. Then I will be dead, like the limb outside my window, broken by the weight of mistletoe, decaying into mulch for next spring. Dead, like the tulips that came up too early this spring and caught a heavy frost last week. Dead, like my dog, whose head I cradled as she closed her eyes and breathed her last breath. Dead, like my grandparents, my parents, and my brother.

What will it feel like?

These hands I've washed thousands of times will not be able to move or to feel slippery bubbles slide off in hot water. The feet that have walked across my tile floors so often will be still, and my ears won't hear the silence of the empty house. No longer will I take off my clothes in the evening and smell the imprint of my day in the garden.

This body defines me. I look at myself and know who I am. From somewhere inside, my spirit peeks out, but it is my body that gives it life, action, words. How will I be recognized without my body?

I came into life kicking and screaming, slippery and hungry. Life was waiting to be lived! Everything lay ahead: so many years to look forward to, the future seemed eternal. Unaware of death, or brokenness, or loss, I was a player in a fairy tale of happily ever after, where every night was opening night and no final curtain would ever come down.

Now, as I grow older, I know that every story has an ending. I see death for the first time, and wonder about my own. Will my mind still think when I'm dead? Will I know what's going on among the living? Will I remember my life on earth?

My grandparents, do they wait for me? Are my dad and mother holding out their hands? And my brother: will we fall into each other's embrace and resolve the differences that held us apart in this life?

Even if I could live forever, I'm not sure I'd want to. I might miss something else, the next phase of life somewhere out there. That place of shadowed dreams and elusive promises I have forgotten since I left. Where is that venue from whence I came? I do not remember.

It is a place words cannot describe, a place no picture could capture. More than anything it is a mystery, a promise we repeat over and over. And in that repetition, we find a mantra of hope, a whisper of the unseen.

To tell the truth, the dying doesn't worry me as much as the how. I've seen too many people live too long and take too long to say goodbye; too much pain at too great a cost.

I've seen grief delayed by medical science, the kind of grief that kills the living as the dying lie suspended by unnatural bondage to life support. These things are worse than death.

When the season of my death approaches, I pray it will be timely. I pray for a gentle passing.

20

Comforter in sorrow,

come to me now.

Speak to my heavy heart

your commitment

to my life

beyond.

A TIME TO PLANT

Planting takes planning: the right soil, sun and temperature; water, mulch and nutrients; perennials for each changing season; color schemes, rate of growth, height. Planting takes thought.

Where shall I plant my family, buy a home, begin a business, find the best schools and doctors and stores? So many decisions to be made before the seasons have cycled even once. So many mistakes easily made without enough information. But decisions must be made. When it's time to plant, it's time to plant.

Seasons don't wait.

So, I whistle a happy tune, try to forget I'm not too sure of myself, and start preparing the soil. I hope daffodils will be happy here next spring. If not, I'll dig them up and plant them somewhere else the following year.

Bulbs are wonderful, storing energy for whatever is ahead. Hidden promises in ugly, onion-like balls. Hidden beauty dressed in flaking shells, ready to surprise gardeners like me. I hope my soul is storing energy for the mystery of tomorrow.

I hope my soul blooms.

Planting takes research and preparation. Soil comes in many stages of readiness, some more receptive than others, some more able to nurture seedlings, some downright unfriendly. I consult nurseries happy to sell me bags of promises, and plants wrapped in pictures. But like all gardeners, I know what it really takes to make a garden: getting down on my knees in the soil, getting dirt under my fingernails, and hurting when I get up. Creating is a dirty job. And a painful one. I ache for weeks during the season of spring.

Planting takes patience and permanence. Patience to wait for the shade of a young tree, for the fruit of a vine and the color of a rose. Permanence to be there when the time is ripe.

Seems I sow more than I harvest. Too often, I am transplanted before I see the work of my hands, or smell the fragrance of fertilizer transformed into a scent of beauty. Without enough time in my garden, someone else will harvest.

Impatience is my partner, yearning for immediate blooms. Hurry, before I'm plucked up again!

I seed ideas into the lives of students and children, and then life takes us in separate ways. I miss seeing them bloom, miss watching them plant seeds of their own along the paths they travel.

Perhaps some of us are created to be planters and others pluckers; some are better equipped to get down on their knees to dig holes for beginnings, while others are better at harvesting.

This I know. Planters need more hope, more trust in the unseen power of growth. Planters know they cannot create alone, and need confidence others will pick up where they leave off, others will nurture the seedlings and harvest the bounty.

The warmth of sun, breath of wind and baptism of rain keep company with those kneeling on the earth, praying, with dirt under their nails.

Creator of roots and stability of soul,

come to me.

Bless the labor of my hands.

Let my garden grow beauty

for those who pass this way

after I am gone.

28

A TIME TO PLUCK UP WHAT IS PLANTED

I have been plucked up too many times.

I've moved into different houses and strange neighborhoods, picked unfamiliar stores and untested schools for me and my children. I have wondered over and over again: Where to place the furniture? Which drawer for the silverware? Is there a doctor nearby? Will the neighbors be friendly? Where is a service station I can trust with my car? Will I like my new job? Who can I call for help?

Moving is questions—where to go for this, where not to go for that. Moving is loss—phone calls and e-mails are no substitute for the face of a trusted friend. Moving is exhaustion—physical, mental, emotional. Strange faces, strange places, endless boxes. Sometimes I sit in the middle of the floor and cry.

My roots have been pulled from the soil where I put them down, where they had settled, where I tended them by hand, protected them from freezing winters, watched for familiar greens to crack the soil each spring, and sadly bade each bloom good-bye as it wearied and took to autumn's rest.

Will my roots transplant? Some won't, and I suffer their demise along with all the other losses and leavings.

To pluck up is to leave behind those places where memories were born. I wander for the last time through my home, remembering holidays in this room, around that table; trees decorated in a certain corner, a window that always caught the morning sun.

To pluck up is to clean for the last time a light switch smudged by children's fingers, to say a final good-bye to a hall, a closet, a hiding place, a squeaky gate, a time-out corner.

To pluck up is to wear yet again that newcomer smile, to offer again that glad-to-meet-you handshake, to try again to remember that forgotten name just met.

Moving happens for all sorts of reasons. Replaced by someone younger, I was moved to a new floor. Promoted, I moved to a new building. Retired, I filled cardboard boxes and moved out of my desk.

Now I am a stranger in a strange land of unknown faces. I am weary of introducing myself to new people, mindful they will never have time to really know me. And maybe not care.

My children are long since plucked up. The nursery is empty. The graduate's room is now redecorated as my office and sewing room. My computer sits on his old desk. The dust makes different lines around my pile of letters.

Now the family room is too quiet, too orderly. I can pick up once a week and arrange the magazines in neat piles. No coats on the floor, no dirty snack plates left by the T.V. chair.

With whom shall I speak? What shall I cook for one? Who will tell me I have lettuce between my teeth? Those intimates have all been plucked up and planted in their own gardens.

Companion in my transitions,

travel with me.

I am a plucked up stranger,

just lookin' for

a home.

A TIME TO KILL

I may be guilty of all sorts of killing and not realize it.

I have never killed another person, but if this gentle mask were removed from the face of my savage soul, then yes, I could kill.

I could kill for my children, for other people's children, for the future. The same things I could kill for, I could die for. Either way there would be killing to save a person or a dream or a nation.

Can love be killed, or does love only die of natural causes? Can love be stabbed or poisoned, smothered, shot, or just bored to death? Am I assisting the suicide of our relationship?

How many more nights will troubled dreams fill the darkness in which love sleeps, or tries to sleep? How many mornings will dawn like a dirge, spreading gray light upon damp pillows and swollen eyes, before love decides to call it a day?

How many times can my heart be killed and resuscitated before love is beyond saving? When is it time to lie down on my slab of memories, and close the door to the morgue?

Some people are more patient and long suffering than I am. Some exist as prey for the hunter, hiding their real selves and delaying the inevitable. And some try to postpone death with all manner of life support.

I am killed by the weight of my unspoken words, by deeds left undone, by my own gifts left unopened. I am ignored, not taken seriously. I feel no worth. My soul begins to rot with loneliness and emptiness and apathy.

I am killed in such subtle ways there are no words to describe the abuse. No witness could see beneath the veneer or read between the lines. I have no case for the courts, no proof, no way to separate from what is killing me and justify my action to others. This thing between us is a secret.

If I turn off my artificial love support, I too must take the blame for my killing. So be it. I will be guilty. I will be the one to say, "Enough."

I awake from dreams, cold and sweating. Troubled sleep drags me through foggy days. Maybe I'm not really alive, or maybe I'm somewhere between the living and the dead. My thoughts cycle endlessly: "What if... I wonder... If only..." I'm stuck; terribly, terribly stuck.

In the meantime, I kill time. This too shall pass, and eventually this dark season will cycle into the next. I will weary of the nausea in my soul, and beg my killing time to be done. Am I a coward, or could I be wise? If I try for one last chance at love, will I miss the one last chance to leave?

I feel I, too, could kill—scratch out eyes, pull a trigger, strangle—but I won't. I will walk tall, work diligently, laugh too loudly, and wait for time to pass. I may dream of accidents and arsenic, but I look for a better way. Not easier, just better.

Then something happens. It may be a small thing, but it is enough to focus me, and I see more clearly. Or it may be a huge trauma, turning me round with lightning speed and making me ask, "Do I really want to live this way forever?"

"No! No! No!"

I find my voice at last, and it is furious.

"This is over! Believe me! It's dead!

~

Comforter in grief and dying,

come with me into the days of my killing.

Bring wisdom.

Bind my wounds with rose petals.

~

A TIME TO HEAL

Quietly, quietly the healing begins. One morning I wake refreshed, feeling lighter, happier. I feel no immediate sadness; then my eyes find their way to a place of memory, and the quiet shadow of my heartache returns. But at least I felt whole for a moment. Then another moment, and another. Enough moments collect to give me hope, and I chuckle.

The sound of my own merriment surprises me the most. I haven't heard myself laugh in ages. It is spontaneous, catching me off my solemn guard, breaking the silence over morning coffee.

As I pour a generous helping of cereal, music tiptoes into the kitchen. Silently at first, then more loudly, the rhythm picks up and becomes a familiar voice. My voice. This is a good sign.

Have I lost weight? I feel bouncy, energized, even bubbly. Whatever the burden was, I am no longer carrying it on my back. Where it went, I have no idea. Nothing of any consequence has happened to change the way I feel this morning. I just feel better.

There is a stirring within my scarred soul, an itching to be tended. And so it is, I begin scratching with fingers of healing, scratching with nails, down my arms and across my back. It hurts so good.

I'm curious again... This is a healthy sign.

I want to get outside myself. I want to enter the world of happenings. I'm tired of contemplating my navel and blowing my nose. Killing has made my world far too small; I want to stretch my spirit beyond the confines of sadness. I want to belly laugh until tears run down my cheeks and I can't catch my breath. I want to explore new ideas, new people, new foods. I'm ready to let go of old pain.

As morning stretches herself across the heavens and throws off a blanket of clouds, I waken with, "Well, Creator, what shall we do today? I've been terrible company for an awfully long time. Thank you for hanging in there and waiting me out."

I'm beginning to dance again, to feel my feet keeping time to an up beat. For too long I have dragged myself around, not seeing the gardens lit by springtime, ignoring the colors enlivening each corner. For too long I have meandered through my days without a place to go, not caring.

Now I can feel melody pushing aside my shroud and taking up residence in my heart. I hear the lyrics of my life starting to rhyme. I want to sing.

I'm beginning to sing.

My soul no longer suffers with laryngitis.

I'm singing!

Once again I'm beginning to laugh the belly laugh of childhood abandon, shaking from head to toe. I taste again. My tongue is alive. Delicious tears wash down my cheeks, christening wounds which no longer sting.

I am healing.

~

Giver of dancing feet, play the tune,

set the rhythm.

Receive my sacrifice of a broken and contrite

heart.

I'm healing now,

and pirouetting in your presence.

~

A TIME TO BREAK DOWN

I am breaking family rules and letting her use my car, even though she isn't paying for the gas or insurance. That was the rule. Was it time to break the rule? It felt right; she's leaving so soon.

She's twenty-five; time for a young woman to leave home and taste life on her own. She's excited about leaving. I'm not sure how I feel, but I know it is time for some things to be broken down, broken open.

We are breaking through the wall in her bedroom to open up space for my office. As we look at the new plans, I try not to smile too much. I don't want her to think I want her to leave, but I will enjoy the extra room. Yes, I will.

It is also time to break down a different wall between the two of us: a fortification I inherited, the wall defending the standards and beliefs of my generation, and my parents' before mine. During our last shouting match, she told me, "I will not accept your rules! I will make my own!"

I love her deeply. She means more to me than any barriers of right and wrong. I will not keep her out. I am ready to break down the barriers of my generation, and to consider the values of her generation. Fewer walls, more gardens.

As the walls come down, we lay a path of stepping-stones, so that we can amble from one garden into the other. Now we meet regularly to sit and chat about things. I don't pry and she doesn't tell me things that might make me uncomfortable. Some evenings when it's cool, we pull weeds and prune away dead branches. Then we cut bouquets for small vases on our desks. These days we laugh a lot, eat chocolates and hold hands before saying goodbye. Our walls exist but they are lower now and we step over them easily.

I think about my parents and grandparents. They had walls of their own, built on fear and distrust of things they did not know: different ideas, different skins, and different speech. They feared their sexuality. They worried about finances—even my finances—because of their own memories of the Great Depression.

Long ago I broke many of those walls down, but in secret; I never discussed my own views with them. I didn't think they would understand. I didn't want to cause a fight. I couldn't stand disappointing them. I was afraid they would stop loving me.

Because of all that, I didn't give them the benefit of my doubt, or my truth.

Now I wonder what would have happened if I had spoken up. I know they could not have changed their own beliefs, the mores of their generation. But would they have tried to understand mine? Would they have loved me more than their rules, and met me halfway?

Perhaps they could have helped me clear a path between their garden and mine, and build a bench where we could have rested and laughed and exchanged the news of the day without judgment.

It's too late to find out. Where they are now, there are no walls, and the only rule is love. But soon, perhaps, we will all share that space, and be able to wander its paths, from one garden to the next.

God of earthquake, wind and fire,

break down the walls of ethical prisons.

Rub stiff necks

so we might bow and pray

on common paths.

52

A TIME TO BUILD UP

I'm building again, feeling free and creative and strong. The breaking down has left me with a clean field. No remodeling around old rooms, no renovations around weight-bearing walls, just starting from the bottom up. I am confined by nothing above the foundation. That's good.

I want to keep the foundation. It was laid long before I was born. Generation upon generation told stories, discussed what worked and what didn't, learned to live together. Through the years of growing toward me, these long-ago people shaped traditions, rules and rituals. Some were good, and built community, and they were kept. Some became divisive and broke the community apart, and they were discarded.

What remains becomes the foundation for the future.

Tomorrow needs an underpinning from yesterday, something to support its unique architecture and possible expansion. Foundations vary, but all fit their purpose: deep cement supports a building; soft quilt fabric supports the appliqué of my grandmother's log cabin designs.

As for me, I rather like a foundation of chocolate cake, moist and dense enough to support chocolate frosting.

Experience teaches me to test a foundation before building. I stroll the surface, carefully at first; then I jump up and down. If it is sure and steady, if it doesn't shake, I mentally place the rooms. I play with the floor plan in my mind's eye, wanting versatile space, natural light, and an entrance big and wide and welcoming – a home for free spirits.

Every foundation needs a dancing test. If I can't dance upon the past, I don't want to build the future on it. I need a foundation to give a little with the high jumps, to support my earthy laughter and spiritual cartwheels.

Only then is it time for the building, the changing and the moving in.

I sit down on my new sofa, put my feet up on the old coffee table and pour myself a glass of Chardonnay. This moment calls for a toast to a job well done. Well done and finished, or so it seems.

Amazing how something else comes up. Too soon, I need to build another addition. Too soon, I'm living in another mess of sawdust and painting rags. Is it ever finished?

I'm beginning to think life is a series of add-ons. Making room for another person here, another idea there; making room for an exercise machine in the spare bedroom or an island in the kitchen. Will it ever settle down?

Making peace with change is my next project. My mental image shifts from houses to ships. I need a vessel that will allow me to move. I will build it with a spacious hull, with room for all the gifts from my past. And it will have a deep and heavy keel, heavy enough to hold me steady as I sail into tomorrow.

~

Master Builder,

help me clear fields and haul off rubble.

Teach me how to fill in potholes

and build altars,

so I might worship in the beauty of

wholeness.

58

A TIME TO WEEP

In the black of night I lie awake and worry. Anxieties waken like night crawlers, to cycle and spiral into deep pits of despair. I am alone, cornered by the memories of shame. I am alone, unable to move or reach for comfort, for someone to hold my trembling. I weep.

Where has all the laughter gone?

I weep because of what I know about life and what I only suspect. I weep for wrong I have done, and for wrong done to me. I mourn the loss of dreams and youth, sunshine and good company, all the happily-ever-afters I promised myself and penned in the diaries hidden at the back of drawers in empty guest rooms. Where has my laughter gone?

I weep.

One day I must get down on my hands and knees, crawl into the dark corners at the back of the closet and pull out all my dirty laundry. Long ago, I threw each item in there, hoping to forget it, hoping someone else would deal with it. But no one did.

It all lay there quietly, only to be resurrected in the black nights of reflection, smelling of shame, disgrace, and heartbreak. Each item needs my touch, the owner's scrubbing, to become clean and new. Each waits for my confession to make it right again.

I will carry those smelly garments to the backyard, toss them onto the grass and begin sorting colors. Stains will need to be treated, then set aside to soak in the baptism of cleansing waters. I will weep over my past.

As my soul shakes out dirty linen and begins to separate garments long forgotten and long outgrown, I reflect on the dirt. The whites are dingy, tainted with dark thoughts. The colors no longer catch the sun and reflect joy. I weep for the bright and shiny days when these garments were new and I dressed myself in laughter.

Why can't I let the past be the past? Why can't I move beyond my shame?

I just can't. And again darkness pushes me into corners of weeping.

As night loosens its grasp and morning peeks shyly into my bedroom, I stretch. I'm grateful darkness is abated for another day.

From my bathroom mirror, swollen eyes blink back. How old I seem. I look away. It's too soon for me to have this face. It's too soon to feel the mantle of age wrapping around my shoulders, or smell the splashing of lavender water. It reminds me of my grandmother. My puffy eyes even look like hers. I don't want to grow old as she did.

Today it's time to launder my soul.

Filling the washtub with soapy water, I pray for cleansing in the font of bubbles. Lifting each garment into the bath, I rub it on the metal washboard. There is a rhythm in the valleys and hills, the bump, bump, bump. My knuckles hurt. I keep rubbing until blood stains the water.

I stop... dry my hands and rub lavender oils into my sores. It kisses my cuts and bruises. Silence waits upon my weeping, and it is no more.

God of quiet step and still small voice,

be present in the shadows of my room.

Wipe my tears.

Whisper to me of heaven.

I have forgotten.

A TIME TO LAUGH

A crack of dawn breaks in through my bedroom curtains. Just a sliver of morning, but enough to lift my spirits after the night. I can feel a salty residue of tears dried upon my cheeks, flaking like summer skin at the end of a day at the beach.

I ponder this moment between darkness and dawn, a symbolic transition between death and life, weeping and laughter, despair and hope. How close they lie together in bed with me. Quickly, I grasp the yellow thread of morning, leave the past upon my pillow, and attend to morning's call.

I pray for joy.

My dog races to the front door and waits. She takes seriously her morning duty of fetching the paper. Dashing toward the driveway, she skids on wet cement and slides toward her prey. I laugh. I laugh so loud, my neighbor looks up as he backs out of his driveway and waves a good morning.

I'm delighted as she struggles with the oversized, Sunday paper. It's just a small chuckle this time, paused on my lips, but encouraging nevertheless. Sections of the paper slip from her bite and litter a path behind her as she runs for the door.

Now merriment has broken the morning's silence, everything seems funny. I laugh at my neighbor's preschooler flapping his arms as he runs, squirrels chasing each other off branches and tumbling to the ground, my cell phone vibrating so powerfully it falls off the table. All these things tickle my funny bone and send me into giggles.

I believe God chuckles – not just occasionally, but frequently. Divine humor is essential to creativity. Taking life too seriously is the devil's duty.

God knows creation as a playful act, an act of the young in spirit. God is very, very old, but very, very young.

God tickles the heavens and they echo with merriment. God coaxes the wrinkles of time to smile by whispering secrets of eternity. God laughs through the very cracks of the firmament into worlds unseen.

We are creatures of this God, fashioned to mirror our creator's mirth. It is heavenly goodness attending our birth that breaks through our first cry, and lifts us to the breast of the divine.

Here we suckle and smack, our mouths curling into smiles. We swallow life and touch the future with curious baby fingers.

As days and weeks and months pass, we chortle at gooey cereal wiped over faces and arms, giggle at Papa's raspberries and belly laugh at Mama's funny faces. Life is good. Life is laughter.

As years and decades dance past, we are invited to laugh at ourselves. I laugh now and feel a deep peace wash through my body, like the waters of baptism. There's something sacred about happiness.

I feed upon the sacrament of joy. I am made whole as I join in God's great, good humor.

My morning prayer is answered.

~

Eternal laughter,

come chuckling into my day.

Bring me the gracious folly

of a chortling spirit,

as I wander

on my way back to

Eden.

A TIME TO MOURN

Friends, family and fellow workers gather in the sanctuary to remember her and to give thanks for her life, and her touch upon each of theirs. Her life was full. Some say she lived many lifetimes in the years she was given. Though she possessed a sharp tongue and wit, she lived with truth and humor and wisdom as her standards.

Those who mourn already grieve the sound of her laughter. She would have laughed as the weather turned wet just in time for her memorial service. Probably said, "The skies are crying my tears, for I will miss you too."

Those who mourn wonder who will speak the truth when politeness and tact finish their speeches. Those who mourn silence their tongues and study the floor, counting the cracks. What can you say of a life like hers? She was one of a kind.

She it was, who often broke the silence with, "Well, what do you suppose would happen if..." or "Oh, for God's sake, somebody tell the truth!"

What would she say today?

Those who mourn wonder where to turn now for the wisdom that moves slowly, thinks kindly, and tells it like it is. Who will be the one to remind us crisis always brings opportunity peeking over its shoulder, or that sometimes life sucks? I wonder who will help us pick up our messes, laughing as we bend over together, trying not to flavor the air?

Here I am laughing and crying at the same time.

Mourning makes my insides ache. Grief catches in my throat. I can't swallow it, or cough it up. It's an emptiness, yet I feel the weight of it. My shoulders sag and my feet shuffle along. How is it emptiness can be so heavy?

I miss her. I miss her sarcasm as much as her soft humor. I miss her patience and her intolerance, her irony and her white lies. She courted truth with whatever verbal tools were needed, but her goal was always integrity.

She died suddenly, right after a fight and before we made up. I am left unfinished, but that's the way we lived: not quite finished. There was always another argument to win, another point to score, at the top of my voice. That's the way we were.

Perhaps this feeling of being unfinished keeps her alive for me. In my mind I continue our disagreement, still trying to win her over to my side. I make notes to show her the next time we meet. Then I remember she is dead, and feel her loss anew.

One morning I wake and think about what I will have for breakfast. I decide on scrambled eggs and English muffins. I think of her death, but not first, and this second thought makes me cry because I fear I am forgetting her.

Forget her? How could I ever forget her? No, she will always be part of me. And I shall always mourn.

~

Landlord of the empty places,

stand with me in grief.

Dry my tears.

Redeem this dirge of mourning time.

Let it not last forever.

A TIME TO DANCE

That's how the dance begins, with a beat.

It begins with a beat. Sometimes it is as soft as my lover's breathing, sometimes as loud as a jackhammer in the street, sometimes as comforting as a grandfather clock.

My body cannot ignore rhythm. It moves, sometimes fast and sometimes not. I sway and hesitate before each step, a New Orleans jazz funeral, a dirge laboring my feet into a slow dance. I kick up my heels, an old-fashioned barn dance, violins and washboards chiding me to keep up. Summer streets burn my bare feet. I jump up and down, skipping toward shade.

It seems to me life is a dance choreographed by God. Dancing lightens my heart. I can't be mean and grumpy or spiteful and wicked when I'm doing the Charleston. Nor can I wage war or plot evil from a chorus line of high steppers.

Our Creator wants us to dance, to live life with light feet, moving with grace upon the earth. We are to dance with the wind, the sun and the moon, to love the creation we are given.

From the beginning, we have been dancers in a garden, skipping through the beauty of an earth unspoiled and very, very good.

I'm an enthusiastic dancer, not a graceful one. If I have a strong partner and the dance is slow, I make it around a ballroom without too many trips. I try to call attention away from my feet with fascinating conversation. Sometimes this works. Most times I feel like I'm dancing in chartreuse when everyone else is wearing black.

All things considered, I prefer watching the graceful movements of others, rehearsed and performing to perfection. I celebrate the ability of dance to leap over walls dividing nations and peoples, the power of its beauty to spill tears from eyes of every color.

The dance of life is where I shine, not because I'm good, but because I'm totally consumed. Choreographed by spirit, my dance is performed in any lively step I choose, any clothes I happen to be wearing, any time of day and any place I find myself glad to be alive.

Each evening as I open my front door, I am an audience for the liveliest dance ever performed, as my Australian Shepherd greets me. Her body quakes with joy, every inch shaking with exquisite abandon. Her doorknob tail shakes with the possibility of kick ball before supper.

When the wind picks up at twilight, my fruit trees dance. Ripe peaches drop to the ground, awaiting my harvest for tonight's cobbler. Zinnias bob up and down, shaking their heads, "Yes, yes, pick me. I belong on your table." Everything alive is moving to the music of the wind. My backyard is a ballroom.

How can I resist?

I kick off my shoes and kick up my heels on cool grass. Arms flinging as wide as my reach, my head falls back to smile at the sunset and I sing at the top of my voice, "I could have danced all night…"

~

God of the beat, Lord of the swing,

hold me in your arms.

Teach me the steps of each new dance,

as my feet follow your path.

A TIME TO THROW AWAY STONES

Which stones shall I cast away?

In the crushing of grain, pieces of soft stone break away, contaminating flour. Soft stones like this, I will cast away. Millstones must be hard, etched with deep ridges, wrinkles from a history of grinding wheat into flour. These stones I honor. These I keep. Only a solid, abrasive surface can grind wheat for my bread.

In my lifetime, this seems to be the way I have discovered each kernel of truth. I am ground and crushed and smoothed. Believe me, I don't like this. How I wish it were easier for me to become wise. I wish I could toss my rigid millstones into the deep quarry from whence they came. But soft stones don't grind useful flour.

Guilt is a soft millstone. It grinds away at my heart, leaving pieces of shame and polluting my creativity. I must forgive myself, and allow a more solid stone to file this rough surface and smooth the hurt I have caused.

An even worse soft millstone is guilt revisited. It grows larger each time I feel the weight of it. My guilt-stone imprisons me with shadowy bars, darkening my day, marking each hour with memories of things I want to forget. I am haunted, emotionally drained. I am sick of feeling sick to my stomach with guilt. I'd like to vomit! Get it all out of my system. Throw it off and fix peppermint tea to freshen the taste in my mouth.

Blame is a stone we cast at others: "If only my mother had... If only my father hadn't... If she had just given me a chance..."

Blame never grows up, never assumes responsibility. It is a selfish adolescent, unwilling to pick up scattered pajamas and half empty coke cans. Blame is an old woman still blaming her wicked stepmother, an old man still blaming the war. When will these stones be tossed?

Hate is a stone with sharp edges. The tighter we hold on to it, the deeper it cuts our hands. Blood drips upon everything we touch, spreading drops of hate like seeds lying in wait for just the right conditions. Seeds of fear and bigotry, suspicion and envy germinate. Apathy fertilizes them. Beware of sharp-edged stones. Toss them far away into places they cannot cut into the future.

On a side table in my office, I have a basket of stones gathered from vacations and walks in the dog park near my home.

They have unusual colors, or strange shapes reminding me of pleasant times. I don't want to throw them away. Sometimes when I'm feeling reflective, I sift them through my fingers and smile.

Now and then I give a stone to a friend who needs to know they are remembered.

"Tuck it in your pocket where you can hear it clicking against your loose change, and let it remind you of my love and support."

Some stones I don't throw away.

~

Lord of all the stones weighing me down,

cut the ties binding me to guilt.

Forgive me, and I shall leap again

kicking up my heels.

~

A TIME TO GATHER STONES TOGETHER

Long ago and far away, they gathered stones and built altars. Those who would worship used what they had: earth, rock, stones. Gathered together, these stones became a place to stop and recognize deities by various names. Some stones were piled as high as the builder's reach, some placed in symbolic patterns. Other altars were but a single stone painted a startling red.

Altars assume an aura of universality. Whether simple or elaborate, each catches the eye of those who pass. Each gives us pause to wonder. Who is worshipped? What prayers are whispered in the passing? Are they answered?

I stop to contemplate the transcendent at a small altar made of sandstone, wondering about life and purpose. Then I continue on my journey, knowing many have preceded me along this path. I am not alone; I am one of many who wonder about those things causing our spirits to breathe with gratitude, to yearn with sorrow, to sing with joy.

I wonder about the children who follow my generation. What will their altars remind them to praise? Who will they stop to thank as they follow their paths? Will their stones be altars or weapons? Will they have the same desires, the same yearnings I have?

Years ago, when I was young and wondering about my roots, I traveled to Arizona in search of my grandmother's brother. Uncle Irvin lived in the desert not far from Phoenix. At the end of a sandy path, I found his name on a sign.

He knew I was coming and greeted me with grace, leading me into a small, three-room house. He offered me water. I accepted.

From a utility pole in the front yard, he powered his refrigerator, a light bulb in the kitchen and a tumbler polishing stones in his bedroom. I wanted to know about the shiny, black Apache tears. He held them out to me in hands as wrinkled as the clay cracking across his yard.

"I'd like you to have these five," he said. "They symbolize tears frozen in time, and offer good luck for your future."

The tears sparkled in my hands, clicking together with soft sounds. He had no idea how many tears were frozen in my past and how much I needed good luck now.

I know I am headstrong and determined. There are those who chide me to throw these stones away, but I won't. I can't. I like the way they shine. They give me energy when I am weary and make me smile when I am overly challenged. I'll keep them always polished, black, rounded. I'll feel them in my palms, rub them together, listen for their murmurings in my pocket.

Someday I shall build an altar of Apache tears. It's fitting, for altars begin with tears and are completed with gratitude. I shall gather stones together after my tears abate and drop peacefully to dry upon the sand. Then piling stone upon stone, I shall build with the bonding of hope.

~

Collector of eternity,

help me build glad altars,

where cracks in the stones

shelter poppy seeds,

ready to sprout and feed my soul

after the next spring rain.

A TIME TO EMBRACE

I have embraced the values of my trade for what seems a lifetime. Schooling and testing and preparing for interviews and then, at last, the job. How proud I was! Co-workers, schedules, office parties, meetings. I relished even the competition, as it proved my worth, my wisdom, my ability to get ahead. Seeing others nod my way, being recognized for what I produced and sought after for my advice. I liked it all. I liked my job. It all fit into my plans and I fit into the world, found a place where I made a difference. I was taken seriously by those I respected, and I began to take myself seriously in the wake of their remarks. Isn't this the way we all want to work?

Embracing company policy, voting the party line, being with the majority – it's good to feel on the inside, part of the "in group". I've grown to appreciate the faces I see each morning, the chatter at lunch, the trust that develops over years together. Marriages and babies and deaths and anniversaries, all celebrated within my work family. It is my community home, dependable, comfortable.

Occasionally, something at the back of my heart feels itchy. This happens when something doesn't sound quite right. I hear a joke that stiffens my smile, a remark that stops me halfway down the hall. I frown. I don't like what I hear. I want to say something or do something, but this is my place of safety and acceptance. I don't want to mess things up.

I leave the scene with a sad feeling. Why didn't I speak up with a corrective? Why can't I be honest with my co-workers? They're my friends. They've been my friends for years. We've been through all sorts of things together. I depend on them when I need help moving into another apartment or picking out a new suit over the lunch hour. I should be able to speak up and voice my opinions as openly as they do. But I don't. I leave feeling slightly ashamed.

The greatest part of my life, I have been embraced by this place, these people, our shared projects. We have developed common goals through decades of working together. And as in a good marriage, we have learned to give and take, to think each other's thoughts and respect each other's point of view. Maybe. Maybe not so much. I'm afraid to find out.

But all in all, I've been lucky! I want to stay in my office, see the same faces when I walk in each morning, know where we will go for lunch and have someone to walk with me to my car at the end of the day.

~

Creator of earth and sea and sky,

bless my work.

Touch the efforts of my head and heart and
hands.

See that they are good.

100

A TIME TO REFRAIN FROM EMBRACING

Even the source of earth and sea and sky rested when creation ended at sundown on the sixth day. Why did I get caught off guard? Did I expect my work to go on forever? Companies change, jobs end, careers are over, retirement looms in everyone's future. I guess all work ends sometime. But after embracing it for so many years, I wasn't prepared for the moment it let go of me.

It feels as though embracing has ended. Now I don't know what to hold close. I have let loose the rhythm of work, the orderly routine of my day, the tick-tock of schedule, knowing the day of the week, the date. I meet new faces and can't remember their names. I meet old faces and sometimes forget theirs. I miss the routine, the way I did things without really having to think. Without routine, time feels strangely empty and disorderly. I've lost the tempo, the work beat. Even the discomforts, I miss.

Now I wish I'd said some of those things I pondered after the fact. I wish I'd let others know how I feel about bigotry and gossip and snide remarks. Now I find the words to say and I have no audience. Shame on me.

I cannot live with a void so full of hours. My day timer is almost empty. How shall I fill my days? When I was working I used a pencil to write on my calendar because things changed so quickly. Now I write in pen because so little changes. I need a reason to get up and dress. I need meaning in my autumn days.

A new beginning takes planning. It's a job to find work. I read the paper, but discover inexperienced college graduates are in greater demand than seasoned professionals. I'm redundant. Imagine – all my years of experience are now a fiscal liability. Today, a whole new approach is needed.

Well, I certainly have time to think about the next move. Let's see: first, I want a task to keep me busy. I want to enjoy it. I want it to have meaning, something I can feel passionate about, keep my mind active and flavor my solitude with imagination.

Adult education classes quicken my curiosity. I've always wanted to know more about photography and genealogy. There is a computer class for digital camera enthusiasts that catches my eye. And a healthy foods cooking lab I want to audit.

I would embrace again those days with things to do, and I'd best keep my pencil sharpened.

104

O, Divine comedian,

make me laugh.

Give me horizons to ponder

and tomorrows to plan

as I listen for new callings

to embrace.

106

A TIME TO SEEK

When I was young, I looked into the mirror and appraised what I saw. I measured myself next to movie stars and models perfectly shaped in pounds and inches. Being a dreamer, I believed the years would give my body better lines, deeper tan and whiter teeth. Being naive, I believed it just took a little self-control and exercise to turn myself into one of the beautiful people I admired. So I worked and dreamed, and was never satisfied with the body of my youth.

Old snapshots of my high school proms, beach parties, and athletic events frame a different picture. I marvel at the fine lines, the healthy flesh, the radiance of high spirits that cast an aura of excitement around me. I had charm, strength and energy. I couldn't see it then. What a pity.

My senior class picture reminds me of the breathless, sexual energy that followed me everywhere, hanging in the air like static electricity. I looked for dates and found them without trying. Clothes hung on my youth with elegance. Abs and muscles flexed with seductive ease. But I couldn't appreciate myself. There was always someone with an inch more or an inch less in places I wanted more or less. Always a more perfect nose, a more engaging smile, a better height. I was seeking perfection. What a pity.

In those self-critical, youthful years I missed the joy of what I had. I let the years slip through my fingers without celebrating myself. In the seeking, I missed the finding.

Adulthood changed my expectations somewhat. I still sought the beautiful people image, still read the movie magazines and looked at body shapes and fashion designs. But I was more involved with others and less into myself. Work and children and friends captured my thoughts and energies. I looked in mirrors and windows as I passed, but my world had become bigger than my reflection.

As scales counted higher and clothes began to shrink, I stood taller and held my breath when I caught someone looking at my waistline. I looked at my friends and found we were not so different. We exercised at the Y and lunched on salads. We talked about the latest diet and even bought the same book on our way home. But usually it lay on my bedside table with only a corner in the third chapter folded down.

Christmas cards stored in attic trunks show healthy, beautiful people. I looked great, and didn't appreciate it.

~

Source of life, give us eyes

to appreciate our reflection.

Shout through the noise of adolescence

and the busyness of adulthood.

Remind us to celebrate the beauty

of our present years.

A TIME TO LOSE

The years mislaid my energy and usurped control of my body. Decades of living seized what I once managed. I used to be fast. "Speedy" they called me. I used to be hungry, could hardly wait for meals. Now I have no appetite. And sex? I smile, remembering my sexual appetite. Every night a banquet. Now I worry about heartburn and leg cramps.

How did this happen without me seeing it coming? Seems like overnight. Wasn't it just yesterday I could sit up till 2:00 a.m. finishing a project and still jump out of bed in the morning? Didn't I take first place just last month, last year? What year was it anyway?

Funny thing about time, as I slow down, it speeds up. When I was young, summer would never come. Now that I'm old, winter's days are dispatched with such swiftness, I am breathless. My green years have run their springy course and now, gray autumn skies beckon me indoors to make soup. And so I do. And it smells good.

Holidays cycle with such speed, I don't take down the Christmas lights hanging from my eaves, or switch my closets between winter and summer clothes. I don't even change my clocks to daylight savings time. In the twinkling of an eye, I'd just have to change them again.

One morning I stretch and yawn in the warmth of early morning blankets. The arms I see above my head belong to a stranger. Wrinkly skin sags from my forearms, giving them a bizarre, elongated wobble. Bruises and liver spots and cuts color transparent skin. Who is this in my bed?

Guess I'd better find out. Guess I'd better make friends with this new person.

Then it hits me. I didn't say "body." I said "person." Rather than looking in the mirror to evaluate myself, I am beginning to look elsewhere. Within.

I don't clean my mirrors any more. I prefer the view from within. Now my Christmas letters feature pictures of

my grandchildren. Words like *grateful* and *happy* and *contented* describe my well-weathered life.

Remembering the years of my youth, all those pursuits, so important then, seem shallow and superficial now. Living my aging, my reservoir of years is filled with thankfulness. I glory in the honesty of my reflections, and find comfort in these wisdom years.

~

Spirit of the ages,

speak to me of what to lose.

Grant me release from the fantasies of youth,

to claim the satisfaction

of my vintage years.

A TIME TO KEEP

When I was a kid, I heard "Use it or lose it," but I just wanted to keep it. New crayons – so beautiful before I wore down their points. New toys – shiny and sleek until my little brother got his hands on them. I put things on a shelf to look at, unused, safe.

In junior high I liked to see my bank balance grow. Other kids dreamed of spending their money, I dreamed of saving mine. I kept stamps, baseball cards, old comic books, never trading anything. I was a keeper.

Dad called me a pack rat; Mother said I was a miser, but I knew there would come a time I would show them how smart I was to keep things.

When I grew up I read, "Things aren't important." But I knew better. I knew clothes and cars and houses and furnishings made me worth knowing, worth being around. So, I kept on keeping.

I also kept things like grudges, and memories of wrongs done to me. I kept a ledger of my own good deeds and another ledger of the bad deeds visited upon me by others. When I was alone, I added them up over and over; I felt good about myself, and resentment toward those who did me wrong. I harbored grudges behind a permanent scowl and pinched eyebrows. Suspicion became my partner and I lost my spontaneity and carefree laughter.

As I grew older I wondered, "Can I keep it? Can I take it with me?" Then I had a dream.

I was at my own funeral. In the front row was a family with strange faces, showing no emotion. The homily was preached by a minister I did not know. I was put in a hole, covered with artificial turf, and all the dry eyes walked away as soon as they could.

There was an estate sale. Everything I kept in life was auctioned off to strangers willing to pay top dollar. My house was sold, the estate settled and then there was silence.

I awoke. There was more silence.

And a terrible emptiness.

Giver of every good and perfect gift,

fill my heart with generosity.

Make me wise.

Show me the difference

between those things worth

using or sharing or giving away.

A TIME TO THROW AWAY

If you move often enough, you learn how to throw things away. Traveling light is easier. Moving fewer things is cheaper. I become reckless as the day approaches when that moving van will pull into my driveway.

The need for haste gives me permission to throw away old books I could have saved for my grandchildren. Old chairs I never recovered. Old clothes I could have used for painting or gardening.

One Thursday before Thanksgiving, I threw away my last pack of cigarettes. Throwing away was easy. Two hours later, keeping myself from digging through the trash ranked as one of the more difficult tasks of my life. Thirty years later, I still yearn for one of those "coffin nails," as my grandfather called them.

Throwing away some things hurts my conscience. I still hear Mother urging me to finish my supper. "Don't make me throw it away! Remember the starving children in China." Years of eating what I didn't want made me fat. And still the Chinese are thin.

Short of a terminal illness, I will never again be able to wear the expensive suits I bought for the office. They hang in my closet getting more dated by the season, but it hurts me to think of throwing them away. Giving them to the local thrift shop soothes my conscience somewhat. At least they will be worn by people who need them.

In years gone by, I threw away relationships too easily and jumped into bed with others too quickly. I burned old yearbooks I'd like to look at again. I gave away my gardening tools when I moved into an apartment, never thinking I might live again in a house with a big yard, never dreaming I would yearn once more for my old trowel.

Throwing away has changed. It has evolved into recycling, reusing, reclaiming. This is the way to be responsible. Inner cities are sprucing up old warehouses into condominiums. Every major city has recycling services. Old and used and previously owned are pronounced good. I want to be recycled.

Black compost bins hide behind bushes in the back of my yard. My grandson delights in the worm factory I fill with table scraps I can't send to China.

During harvest my town shares fruits and vegetables, bartering organic gifts planted and tended by our own hands.

This makes me happy.

Provider of all time and space,

throw away the unnecessary in my life.

Then grant me wisdom to save the precious

and recycle what needs

a second chance.

A TIME TO TEAR

There's something violent in the sound of tearing. Sight unseen, you know exactly what's happening. You know something is ripping in two. Intentional or not, it will never be the same. And deep in my stomach a question is twisting: But will it fix? Will it ever fix again?

One afternoon, returning home from school, I heard my mother tearing cloth. She was sitting by the window, ripping the hem out of my sister's dress. Mother was crying. Her youngest child would never be this short again.

The crease line of the first hem would always remind Mother of earlier days, simpler days when my sister's world was smaller and safer, and she found comfort in Mother's lap. The more crease lines there were – worn into the fabric by iron and dryer – the more complicated my sister's life grew. Like the rings of trees, her hemlines marked her growth. And finally she needed a new dress.

The sound of tearing tells a story of growing up and out and into places mothers cannot mend. Those crease lines remind us of the past, the sheltered, fixable days of earlier years, when there was someone to take care of us – before we got yanked around by people who didn't love us or know us or care to. Before we got jerked around by school or job or finances, there had been safety in coming home after school and smelling cookies baking the moment we opened the front door.

Tearing leaves me unsettled. Letters torn in half can be taped back together, and tears in my clothes may be mended, but when I lose my temper and tear into my child, can I mend this? No, not like new, never like new again.

My country torn by war, social issues and inequality – will these tears ever be patched? Can we grow into the future with only crease lines reminding us to be civil and just and kind? How gentle a reminder this might be.

The grayer I grow the more torn I feel. I waken some days emotionally scattered by mental errands pulling me in every direction. There are holes in me no one can see, runners and splits and seams ready to burst. I am torn into so many pieces.

On the outside, I look pretty good for my age. No one would ever guess how deeply I yearn to have my hem let down again.

~

Hand of God,

take needle and thread to my shredded life.

Gather all my scrappy pieces,

and stitch me together again.

A TIME TO SEW

Dad wakes, and rolls over on his side. From my chair at his bedside, I glance up, but his gaze shows no distress. "It's so comforting to see you sewing," he says.

My dad is dying. As I sit with him, I am stitching on a quilt I tucked away long ago, planning to finish when I had a break in my schedule. I will still be sewing at the moment – three weeks from now – when Dad takes his last breath. His final task complete; mine unfinished. I lay it down, push my needle into the fabric and cry.

Strange how the simple things become important at the end.

I loved my dad deeply. During the years he served overseas in World War II, I prayed every night for his safety; only when he came home did we feel like a family again. Knowing he admired academic scholarship, I studied hard, ultimately earning my doctorate. He enjoyed my high profile profession; I rose in my job to address thousands. He was proud of my friends and connections. I wanted to please him. I did.

"It's so comforting to see you sewing," he said.

On my office walls are framed diplomas, honorary degrees, and pictures of me alongside famous faces. They hang slightly crooked. I straighten, dust and remember.

In earlier days, he would come into my office, straighten the framed benchmarks of my life, stand before each, smile and sigh. At the end he watches my hands push needle and thread through cotton colors, and smiles as he falls asleep.

Scraps of material gathered over the years comfort me too. They give me something to do with my hands while I wait; something homey and familiar to touch, as I remember the living gone into each piece of cloth...dresses, robes, formals, even a few scraps from old pajamas. My children wore some of these materials. Hardier clothing passed to

smaller children until there were no more children, only an unfinished quilt. The smell of baby powder lingers on soft pastels.

Sewing these pieces together creates patterns, making a simple sort of sense out of my life. Some of the patterns don't blend and some of the colors clash. That's my life. I wore all the pieces when they were whole garments, and yet I didn't feel whole.

But, strangely enough, as these pieces stitch together, I see patterns emerging and I feel more complete.

Dad's death puts things in perspective. Comforted by the sight of my fingers moving up and down, in and out, creating a methodical rhythm with the scraps of my life, he slipped into his next.

The last time I kissed Dad, he said, "Take a piece of my old work shirt and sew it into one of your designs."

Creator of life's design,

hold a quilting bee over me.

Take pieces from my past, and

stitch a new pattern

into my tomorrow.

A TIME TO KEEP SILENCE

Silence screams when violence is ignored. The violence of poverty, hunger, molestation and greed. The violence of word and deed. What seems peaceful for lack of explosion or marching is the stillness of fear, the hush of dark secrets, the calm before storm troopers knock, before the sound of angels weeping.

Silence smiles as we stand back and let the little ones figure out a puzzle or wait upon the old ones to remember a word. The gentle silence of waiting upon others encourages autonomy, demonstrates respect.

When silence throws in the towel and refuses to engage in healing conversation, it has a grim power. Stifling dialogue, it protects the status quo. It holds the key to beginning again and refuses to unlock that possibility. It responds passively, "Nothing's wrong. And if it is, I can't do anything."

Sometimes I teeter on the brink. Should I speak or not? Will it help? How should I say it? And sometimes I get sick of having to choose my words so carefully; all spontaneity is lost. I wish I could just blurt out what I'm feeling.

When I was a child, I spoke with a child's honesty, and discovered truth is not always acceptable among certain people. I learned to edit what I said. Parents and teachers told me I was showing maturity and tact, but now I wonder if I was only learning to tell white lies.

Silence can be the greatest offense and the greatest compliment.

Kindness is spoken through silence too. When I have no words in the presence of deep grief, I am silent. I stand close and touch tears. When a friend needs companionship to unload secret burdens, I am silent. I sit close and hold eye contact. When someone wants to apologize to me, I am silent. I stop everything to honor their confession with deepest gratitude.

Awe is silent. Mixed with reverence and amazement, awe catches me off guard in the presence of shocking sunsets, the smell of my baby's neck, frantic puppy kisses. What can I say in the company of greatness. Words are never enough in the presence of incredible art, or literature, or my lover?

Only sighs.

~

Word of God, speak through me

when silence is wrong.

Touch my mouth with the wisdom of your still,

small voice and give to my silence

your words.

A TIME TO SPEAK

Shall I speak? Her tests came back positive. Do I tell her the diagnosis, the truth about her chances? How much truth? When?

I plan to leave him soon. How do I tell him? What words can I use to explain why I don't want to be with him any longer? Do the reasons make any difference after I say good-bye? Is there a way to save his face and ease my guilt? I don't know what to say, but I need to say something.

What is truth, when it speaks shattering information? I try for the right words and no matter how I say it, my feelings win. I discover truth is feelings more than facts. I hear truth differently than someone else. My truth-ears filter words through my experience and translate them with the help of my emotions. There is no universal truth.

In sorrow, truth hangs heavily around my shoulders, yoked to darkness and dread. In joy, truth dances ahead of me, pointing out the wild flowers and newborn bunnies.

When hope speaks, it tells the truth. It may speak of sorrow, but never sorrow in isolation. In the same labored breath, hope speaks of possibility. Thus, when hope speaks, we can suffer the slings and arrows of factual bombardment, for there is always more to hear. Options, choices, plans and dreams.

When truth speaks with smiles, facts dance and sing for joy. When smiling truth is shared, there is fellowship. The war is over! The surgery was successful! You have a son! The lost is found! When truth speaks with smiles, even sad news is easier to hear and understand. The heart doesn't race for long. Panic breathes deeply again.

Ecstatic truth shouts, casting an enchanting spell, welcoming even strangers to toast each other and celebrate good news. Silence is impossible. Even stones cry out in delight.

When we speak with compassion, all are comforted: those who suffer, and those who remember times they yearned to hear such words.

Glad truth binds enemies with common words, changes scar tissue into baby's skin, whispers, "Forgive me," and plows through dry and tired fields. Glad truth readies old soil for spring planting.

~

Kindly voice, give words to my mouth

and meditations to my heart.

Render unto me truth with hope,

silence with sympathy, and

speech with grace.

A TIME TO LOVE

I want to love again. I want to feel light and bubbly, to hear laughter burst once more from the emptiness inside me. I want to feel that rush of adrenalin when I hear, "I love you." I want to be the one that somebody is thinking about in the pauses of a busy day, the face they can't forget, and the body they yearn to touch. That's what I want.

And little by little, the time is ripe. It's time to love and be loved again. I'm worn out waiting. My skin is lonely. I want someone to spoon with at night and wink at in the morning, someone who touches me for no reason at all and tells me my extra pounds feel good. I want to love with abandon, without fear of offending or worrying about holding my stomach in when we make love.

Love is getting a speeding ticket rushing home to tell the latest joke. It's opening the mail together with a glass or two of wine. My spirit needs a friend. I want a soul mate.

Love changes everything. My metabolism speeds. My face lights up and holds a warm blush all day. The clock runs too fast when we're together and too slow when we're apart. Breathless whispers. Skipping steps. Music. Office windows reflect silly grins fixed upon my face. I forget to breathe.

The electricity I feel is far from static. Lightning cracks and I feel I can do anything: run a marathon, get the job, lose fifteen pounds, write the next great American novel, win the lottery. You name it, I can do it! Nothing's impossible.

And yet this is only half the picture. The other side of love is quiet, comforting, enfolding. Winter is cozy as blizzards attack. Summer breezes cool record-breaking heat. Spring rains promise violets. Autumn colors soften yards for Saturday afternoon tumbles.

This I want: the shouts and the whispers, the frantic rush to jump in bed and the slow stroking of my belly. I want it all.

Love enduring through illness and grief makes sweet the valleys of life. Love supporting in times of terror, holding hands during the evening news, weeping together when war clouds gather. There is a depth in this kind of love, rooting deeply and growing with perennial hope. Together, we can endure.

This love waits. It waits for bad times to move on and better times to drop by and stay awhile. It struggles in tandem to escape the quicksand of today's world and skips words of support across rushing rivers. Love finds curdled milk in the back of the refrigerator and takes it out of the oven as hot buttered biscuits.

~

Creator of erotic joys for human flesh,

praise be to you,

for the climax of body and soul

after desert days of emptiness.

~

A TIME TO HATE

Something is seething inside me. I am so full of it I can't think. From the growling pit of my stomach it rises. I christen it hate.

How can I hate my beloved, the one I married on a summer day of champagne and roses? From where does such outrage come? How can I hate my country, the place I was born and raised, and couldn't wait to come home to? How can I hate myself so easily, just by looking in a mirror?

The ferocity of my emotion frightens me. Time to take a deep breath and forget what just happened. Right! That's a joke! I'm always trying to forget unpleasant things and it never works. I toss them to the wind and like boomerangs they circle round and hit me from behind, just when I thought they were gone.

I try exercise, to work off steam, and end up exhausted and still hateful. I try thriller movies, to voice-over the shouting matches in my head, and can't concentrate on the plot. Sleeping pills don't make the nights any shorter, and when I pick up my novel, I find myself reading the same paragraph over and over.

How can I exorcise hate?

Perhaps I need to sit with it and let the course be run.

I know I need to stop and ponder the part I might have played to dig this chasm, but I'm still defending myself. I must feel safe before I can let down my guard and be vulnerable before my demons. I can't analyze all the possibilities if I'm not willing to lay everything on the table and be honest with myself. I must wait. I'm not ready.

It's okay to hate for a while, if it's part of a process and not the end product. I've learned the longer I have to wait on my readiness, the greater the depth of attack. I've discovered forgiving too soon is wasted energy and never lasts, only festers. Forgiving too soon leaves unfinished business.

   If I don't do this forgiving stuff in a timely way, it will come back to haunt me passively disguised in smiles. I think I'll hate for a while and wait to see what happens. Something must. I grow so weary of this burden.

~

Giver of every passion,

feeler of every emotion,

help!

Lift the nausea of hate filled separation.

Lengthen my days

and shorten my nights.

166

A TIME FOR WAR

War's uniform has many pockets. Blood and death, bones and bombs spill out of one. This pocket wants to be forgotten, to be buttoned down as ancient history, never to be emptied again – the horror of memories visited only in nightmares.

Another pocket holds pictures and letters from home, beloved faces smiling through the sorrow of separation, familiar script and preschool drawings. A love letter, a poem written and illustrated in a fourth grade classroom, a wedding invitation from a friend who will have to send pictures. This pocket is warm and worn and stitched right over the heart.

Unfamiliar coins and unknown tongues clink and chatter in yet another pocket. Peculiar languages isolate. Stumbling over the correct change, the right word and the pronunciation of eccentric names make me feel at risk. Simple, ordinary tasks take three times as long in strange neighborhoods, and the constant fear of violence jumbles clear thinking and detours my focus. I feel misplaced, stupid and very, very vulnerable.

One pocket holds songs, carried into the night on bawdy voices of tipsy leave-takers. Voices cheer the darkness of blackout and make brave attempt to drown out the noise of battle. Earphones and iPods sing of Christmas and country roads. Rap and jazz and rock comfort worn bodies.

There are pockets filled with M&Ms and cigarettes and gum. Not as many cigarettes as soldiers carried in wars past, but more candy. Children see it and little feet follow, running and pointing at bulging pockets. Small friends are made for tomorrow's world, because children remember chocolate.

"Just-in-case" letters are folded with names and addresses, stamped with the prayer they will never be mailed. Dog tags rattle in another pocket. They tap out the rhythm of hope.

Should wings of peace hover close, and brush my cheek with a branch of the olive tree, I will race to be wrapped in the embrace of armistice. That will be the time for turning out my pockets and viewing the collection stored in my fatigues. What shall I save? What will make for soul peace and what will make for consoling memories? What is best put back in a pocket, folded up in my uniform, packed away in a footlocker and carried into in the attic?

Lord of horse and chariot,

foxhole and home front,

grant your weary soldier

no more time for war.

Fill my pockets with bulbs

for planting daffodils.

A TIME FOR PEACE

When the laughter of a wee one rains upon the smolderings of war, and embers melt into rich earth ready for spring planting, there is peace.

When morning stretches herself across the sky, reaching to embrace the dawn; when creatures waken in warmth to celebrate another day, there is peace.

When refugees wander onto welcoming lands, begin building homes and find a safe place to birth their young, there is peace.

When we practice our creational bonding by naming and feeding and bathing the beasts, there is peace.

When we do not rush, but instead take all the hours we need to complete a task well; when we receive the gift of time's fullness, yet acknowledge the numbering of our days, there is peace.

And so, if I would be a peacemaker, it is my heart I first would pacify.

Breath of God, breathe on me. Blow out my fires of revenge. Light the wick of wisdom's oil, and let me be your light in the dark corners of our world's despair. Give me springtime energy to step lightly into the green fields of home, to plant trees, compose songs, honor the earth and restore its beauty from the ashes of war.

Give me understanding for those returning from war whose eyes have seen too much blood and ears still echo with screams. Give us time to sit and reason together, to weep and remember, to listen with the grace of silence, the warmth of compassion and the soft touch of a hand.

And when, a distant trumpet begins to play, wakening a day of peace, may I smile dawn into my heart. May I find contentment in simple things that make for peace.

When my senses celebrate old songs in the making of new memories, when a hamburger with fries is the best meal in the world, when my favorite chair enfolds me, there is peace. And when the scent of love leaves me breathless and tears fill my eyes as I gaze upon a healthy child running down the street, there is peace.

When at my death there is a smile upon my face and the earth smiles back, there is peace. Until then, with our swords beaten into plowshares, let us till our fields and feast; let us birth our babes and celebrate their weddings with song.

~

God of song,

play me as your instrument

in a symphony of peace

Give to me your lingering refrain through

my earthly days,

and a pillow of peace for my head at night.

Shalom.

Notes about the Author

Sylvia Casberg received her Masters of Divinity and Doctor of Ministry degrees at San Francisco Theological Seminary. During the 1980's and 1990's, she served congregations in Denver, CO and Moscow, Russia.

She traveled the Middle East to research, photograph and write the book, "Serving the Least of These," for the Presbyterian Church (USA).

In 2001, she was called as a chaplain to the University of Colorado Hospital in Denver. After the birth of her grandson, she moved to Solvang, California. Here she formed the Sunny Fields Publishing Company.

Sylvia is now writing, publishing and grand mothering.

www.SunnyFieldsPublishing.com